first of all, i'd like to thank god for this opportunity, for life, for everything. never would i have imagined that people would be holding my words, my thoughts and emotions, my pain and happiness in their hands in paper form, so thank you. i am ever so grateful for your continuous love and support and i pray my words help you, that you fall in love with them. thank you to my family, to my friends, to the writers of instagram, every beautiful friend I have made from the platform, to the people that have come, and the people that have left. thank you for keeping me alive, thank you for keeping me sane. to whoever is reading this, you are in my prayers, may happiness and love fill your life, may peace find you. this is the start of something beautiful.

-   Faisal

Contents:

affection

this chapter about my life is about love, several types of love from different people. i don't know if i've ever been in 'love' in terms of someone who isn't family, yes, i've had my share of relationships but i guess they were all a lesson to bring me to today, to bring this book to you. the poems in this chapter revolve around my past relationships, different poems relate to different people, my mother, my late grandmother and loving yourself. love is a big part of life, it's a foundation upon which everything springs, and it's vital for us to love ourselves before we welcome love, before we try to understand its mystery. i've learnt not to chase love but to let love chase you, to let it find you for it'll come when you're ready, mentally, emotionally and spiritually. i have been in love with moments and places, hence my words contain so much emotion for in those moments and at those places i felt love, i felt it for a moment, and before it left i managed to capture it. so read on and hopefully it'll spark something within.

affection

you whispered honey and i fell in love with its sweetness, i wrapped myself in your words to keep the winter away. my hands would tremble at your touch, my skin felt weightless, you touched my insides and loved what mattered. i felt the softness of the clouds and the warmth of the sunshine when you looked at me, this was love. you loved me when i wasn't so loveable, you took me home, you made a home inside of you and i clutched your hand so tight in fear one of us will let go. no wonder why i always remember you, for many made me smile but you were the one that found it.

-    why love came.

affection

my mother is the strongest woman i know,
her hands are like steel but her tongue is as soft as a feather.
a single mother
who raised three boys and made them men,
lions who become cubs when she speaks.
a woman who
feasted on her own tears so we could dream,
who fasted from the luxuries of life,
just so we'd understand how it feels to smile without worry.
she is the foundation of who and what i am,
my heaven lies under her feet,
my world lies with her.
i pray i am half as strong.

- my mother.

affection

your smile
is the most delicate colour
i have ever seen.
let me fill your life with rainbows,
i will adorn the stars
around your neck
and the moon
inside of you.

-     that smile of yours.

affection

please i plead
do not become a
stranger to me,
for you are the
air in my lungs,
you'd make both of us
collapse.

- do we depart?

affection

had i let the ocean
know of our love,
i swear
its waves would stop,
the tide would sing for you,
the horizon would chase us,
its shells would follow.

- ocean love.

affection

the simplicity of all that you are
encapsulated me,
the way salt absorbs within water,
we form one.
we became the ocean,
your love gave us life.

- saltwater.

affection

i wept as tear drops fell
down my cheeks,
i prayed for your happiness
through the weeks,
i hoped you'd receive
all of mine,
love is like this,
i pray you're fine.

- we show love through prayer.

affection

in all honesty, i wouldn't know, for i have not been in love. i have been in love with the idea of love, in love with places, memories and moments but maybe never entirely with a person for lust clouds my vision, but maybe i am wrong. i'd say it works in the fact that your other half becomes part of you, they live within you, with all their happiness and sadness, the good days and the bad days. love works in sacrifice, in understanding, in acceptance and negotiation, laughing until your stomach hurts and so much more. it works through prayer, faith, trust and resilience, every emotion that finds home under the night sky. it is impossible to describe the way love works, for we don't know how it feels until it truly hits us, and love is different for us all.

- how does love work?

affection

they ask,
'does it hurt when you think of them now?'

i reply no,
you see, you look back at memories,
glad that out of seven billion people and growing,
you two were chosen to share those moments,
just you two, and that's beautiful, right?
and as time passes you understand why
everything happened the way it happened.
you realise that hurt is growth,
and growth is strength,
and strength brings us to today.

so, no, when i think of them
i see the growth i've made to
come to today,
not the fact we lost our all.

- when they ask.

affection

22nd february: 'i don't understand how everything got so messy'
5th march: 'you don't need to try and make me feel better'
6th march: 'i'm sorry'
18th march: 'don't do anything to hurt yourself please'
31st march: 'i'm glad we're okay'
7th april: 'you hurt me loads'
15th april: 'you okay?'
20th april: 'idk why but that make me laugh'
22nd april: 'i'll annoy you another day *laughing emoji*'
22nd may: 'just ignore me and pretend i don't exist'
22nd may: 'i can't stop feeling the way i do and you hurt me so damn much'
11th june: 'i'm okay'
15th june: 'you're always in my prayers'

you see, these are all real texts. break-ups are messy, they are conflicted, they consist of good days and bad days but in the end, you both move on, you both heal. we fail to understand the importance of time, how time heals scars we cannot see. sometimes we can't heal others, actually most of the time we can't, we just have to let god, the universe and time do their thing so keep them in your prayers and understand that despite your world collapsing, you won't collapse completely, you'll heal and get past your pain. and to all those i've hurt, i pray you forgive me. as humans, we are defined by how we react to our mistakes, not our mistakes. you cannot heal everyone, it doesn't matter how much you try something things and people need to break, it's destiny.

- thirteen messages you sent me

affection

you are a paintbrush
so gentle in your technique,
a perfect brushstroke
as you paint life so warm.
you are so vibrant in your colours,
you can paint our story,
colour it with love.

- paintbrush.

affection

her voice
bubbles like champagne
and i became intoxicated
until i forgot what love
tasted like,
you made me forget.
you were my drug.

- champagne love.

affection

i hope the city lights shine as bright as you, the way they illuminate across the darkness of the sky. the city is full of chatting lovers and beeping taxis, the distant sound of children playing and hope which echoes through the forgotten atmosphere. there are sky-high buildings of plummeting conversations and the howl of emotions which make it hard to breathe the already polluted heartbroken air. when will you learn that you are my city, that your words carve roads and your touch is the map to guide me so trace my fingers down your back, let's get lost in the city, let's go to places we've never been before, for every part of you is my home.

- city lights

affection

can you not see
how these half crescent moons
curve to mimic your smile.
keep smiling my beloved,
please never stop.

- half-moon.

affection

when i say i am going to pray for you i am going to do the following five things.

1.) pray for your mountains of sadness to become weightless clouds and disappear into the skies of your mercy.
2.) pray that your wishes come true, that the words which pour like rivers from your lips are answered by the almighty.
3.) pray that the blessings of the almighty rain upon you, may it rain and may it never stop, may you drown in his blessings, and let me drown with you too.
4.) pray that the almighty protects you from the harm of the world and most importantly the harm we cause ourselves.
5.) pray that we are united, if not in this world then in the next, for i shall love you in both.

- praying is how we love.

affection

the night whispers to my beloved
when her hands are cupped in prayer,
as she whispers for me.
your forehead is planted to the earth,
parallel to the lines of the night sky.
your palms are still like the moon,
but it doesn't shine as bright as you.
you sacrifice your happiness for me,
you give up your moon,
for my light,
this is love.
love is like the space between
the moon and the stars,
infinite.

- she whispered to the moon.

affection

you are beautiful, ever so beautiful and uniquely created, no eyes could ever match yours nor could any soul. we are all beautiful in our different ways, both inside and out. never let anyone tell you that you aren't beautiful, don't let them convince you that your eyes are too wide apart, or that the hair on your face makes you ugly, don't let them compare you to anything or anyone else. i know you spend hours looking into the mirror, picking out the tiniest of flaws and overthinking them, but you have to learn to love yourself, because at the end of the day you're all you have. someone will come and love and appreciate you so don't change for the world. we all have our own flaws and insecurities but that what makes us human, that's what makes us normal. you are beautiful, you are, you are, you are. love the little things about you, love the silly things you do. yes, it's easy to say and so much harder to do, but always remember that you were created in perfection, and without you the world would not be the same, there is beauty in your smile, hope in your eyes and love inside of you, please remember and believe that.

- self-love.

affection

sometimes
i ponder over why
god bought you back to him,
asking why my anchor had to leave?
but now i say,
why not me?
for i long to be re-united with you,
as we smile,
as you live pain free,
as you live happily,
and that gives me peace.

- why you?

affection

gardens of green bloom for you, the petals that make love to the rose overlap to conceal your beauty. its thorns keep those who try to harm you with their lust filled words away, may you always be protected from harm. the leaves bring life, the way your smile breathes resilience into me. the blood red of the petals stains my fingers when i lay my warm hands on your cold skin, i trace them over your goose bumps. it is either the sign of my sin or the longing for us to bleed into another world where our love exists.

- love lies in the garden.

affection

rose thorns
dance in my veins,
it hurts to breathe,
i have forgotten how to.

- what happens when we wish for thing
  that will never happen.

affection

1.) i asked if you had eaten several times during the day, i always knew you had but i wanted to make sure, neither of us wanted you to go back to your past.

2.) squeeze your hand tighter than usual when you were sad, this was to let you know that i will never let go, that maybe ever the world could not pull us apart.

3.) prayer. i prayed for you through the passing days and blissful nights. i knew how much you were aching and that only god can help, so i went directly to him.

4.) they kept talking about how we'll never survive yet the only thing i believed was your words. though they were right, i kept my faith in you, in us.

5.) i could listen to your stories all day, i was addicted to you and all you had to say, tell me everything. i want to know every detail that makes you who you are.

6.) i saw you beneath your outer beauty, i wanted to hear your thoughts and fall deeper in love with you, to have something physicality could never fulfil.

7.) i would give you my all and fight the universe for you, i swear i would have if you had let me.

-   seven ways i said i love you.

affection

my love for you
runs like a river.
the tide chases you,
for you are a horizon,
which calls me.
i would drown
if it meant
we'd unite.
my love is such

-    river love.

affection

your eyes. they were brown and i know how they say brown is boring, brown is muddy and dirty, full of imperfections, incomparable to the tropical nature of the blues and greens. don't get me wrong, the blues and greens are beautiful but nothing beats brown eyes. your eyes are brown like the sand of the desert, like the soil which gives life to the world, it is enriched with so much love, so much that your pupils dilate whenever you smile, as though you are dying for others to smile with you. there is mercy in those eyes of yours, there is compassion embedded within those eyes which turn hazel brown in the warm sunlight and pearl black in the darkness, where only the moonlight can guide us. brown is the most beautiful for the mystery it holds, for the way you have to look deep down to find its secrets, the way you have to unravel those secrets through putting together the whole puzzle of the rest of your body. your eyes are brown like the thick cotton women adorn in my hometown, they are brown like brown has always been my favourite colour, like brown is the only colour i see on the palette. your eyes are brown and they are beautiful.

- brown eyes.

affection

all the words
in every language
to every exist,
would still not
be enough to
describe the
happiness i
feel when i
see you.

- languages.

affection

i wish the world did not revolve around appearances. love comes from within but it finds home on the outside. your soul is a hundred times more beautiful than your body or any of your physical features. now that isn't because you aren't beautiful on the outside, you are, believe me, it's because your soul was what drew me closer to you. just because we can't see the soul, does not mean it should not be appreciated, and that's why we end up appreciating faces and misplacing love to come from beauty.

- inner love.

affection

i pray every day that it is you
written for me.
may our paths be drenched
in the rains of destiny,
may your name be carved in stone
right next to mine.
and of all of god's blessings,
you are the most divine.

-     my wish.

affection

i love you, i love you the way the moon loves the night sky, the way it floats so effortlessly, dressed in lust as it leaves when it leaves, comes when it comes. you make me happy on the days i cannot find the strength within me to smile. i pray everyone else in this hurt world finds someone with a fraction of the kindness and love you show to me. no metaphor underneath this shadowed night sky could describe your smile or that glow in your eyes when you fall into your fit of laughter. you are the epitome of beauty. your sweet nature has changed the cruel adult within me into a sweet child, every lyric of those cheesy love songs now make sense, they are tattooed under my skin. the sweet sonnets of poetry i read leave your name echoing in my head. you are something special and so much more. i am totally intrigued by your character, lost in your conversation and your intellectual nature which makes me fall more in love with you every time our minds connect. i wake up every day eager to talk to you and fall asleep every night eager to wake up to you. you've put a definition to the word happiness in my heart, i cannot stop smiling, my face hurts. i pray we are united in this world and the next, that i have the privilege of loving you for an eternity, to hold your hand on the good days and bad days, to understand you to the best of my capability. i now understand the language in which the birds fill the morning sky, the melody of the warm sunsets, the poems written in the blood of red roses, it all finally makes sense to me. thank you for turning my tears into laughter, my darkness into light. i love you.

- love letter.

affection

i love you.
for no words
could ever say more,
than these three.

- final love poem.

<u>write down five things that help you when you're feeling down:</u>

1.)

2.)

3.)

4.)

5.)

breaking

this chapter is about my breaking, how the world has hurt me and how i have hurt myself. as someone who is diagnosed with depression, anxiety and a personality disorder, living everyday had become a struggle and it's so much harder being a teenager lost in this world. when family problems, relationships, social pressures and just the general everyday feeling of being down come together, it becomes messy. i attempted suicide twice during april 2016 and all praise to god i survived. here i highlight how i broke, how i completely collapsed with no hope of putting myself together again, but here i am writing this, a reminder to you that we all pull through. i also speak about living with a single father as my parents have been separated for 11 years and officially divorced for about a week as i'm writing this. i also lost my grandmother five months ago, and the losing of a loved one leaves open a void that sometimes only time can heal. we all hurt, we hurt in different ways and different intensities but we all go through something, i hope my words give you the comfort you are searching for, understand you are not alone.

breaking

i was told there is good
in each of us,
but they forgot to tell me
some have more bad.

-      masks.

breaking

i squeezed her hand so hard
in hope, it felt like yours.
and now i have marks on my hand
like the ones on my skin,
but those won't disappear.

-     hand prints.

breaking

my tears
have stopped flowing,
it is too kind
to let them fall,
i let my insides drown.

-    lungs full of tears.

breaking

my anger became silence
and that became sadness,
it wrapped its arms around me
and sung poetry and sweet songs.
my sadness expressed its love
and i begged for her to leave,
yet she clings onto me
like a new-born baby,
the only difference is that
it's me who cries.

- sadness why won't you go?

breaking

what is intoxication?
how can i ever overdose
when i have loved
the way we did.

- no limit.

breaking

may every tear that falls from my eyes
be a blessing that falls for you,
i just wish you the best,
and hope the good times call me too.

- guilty feelings.

breaking

you said you loved
the little things about me,
is that why
you made me feel so small?

- little things.

breaking

if only we knew
that these moments
would only last for moments.
how foolish were we
to believe a love like ours
would last a lifetime.

- fools for love.

breaking

often when we look back into our pasts, evaluating the type of person we were and how different we are now, we fall onto the topic of the people who used to be in our lives and how they are no longer here. you. you've always been the first that comes to mind, your name lives on the tip of my tongue, it dances inside my mouth but it is too afraid to leave. it's always been you and it will always be you, the one who i cannot forget, the one my memories ache to let go off.

- it was always you.

breaking

every day late nights
all sleep day time,
asking you why,
why did you leave?
where are your promises
because it is three am,
and you're the only thing
on my mind.

- late nights.

breaking

i had my first heartbreak, and my worst that aches my chest to this day, around 11 years ago. a young boy needs his father, he needs someone to teach him to become a man, to help look after the family and to complete it. there is this emptiness within me that i still cannot heal, how i grew up with a void in my life, a role which held a title but none worthy to be an occupant. my mother has shed enough tears to fill the skies, my siblings have asked as many questions as the earth has trees and i have blamed myself enough. your absence cracked foundations we could never repair.

-      my biggest heartbreak.

breaking

when a loved one dies you hold their belongings in your hands but suddenly these boxes full of medicine feel empty, these colourful scarves feel grey, everything reminds you of them. when a loved one dies your heart physically aches for you to remember them, those bold brown eyes, golden wrinkles, hair dyed in mendhi, you pray your picture-perfect memory will never let you forget the small details a photo cannot capture. when a loved one dies you remember the last time you spoke and if you expressed your love you will sigh in relief and if you didn't you'd shed a tear, wishing you did. you'll then whisper, 'i love you' and pray that through god they'll somehow hear it, but i'm sure they already knew, they loved you too. when a loved one dies it feels as though time freezes, you come to terms that you'll never hear the melody of their voice calling you again, or the sweetness of their sugar-coated arms wrapping around you, and sometimes it takes months or even years to come to this acceptance. when a loved one dies, you remember all the things they did and said, you remember what they loved and what they didn't, you remember all the memories you shared. when a loved one dies, so does part of you.

i miss you, and i'll continue to do so for an eternity.

- when a loved one dies.

breaking

you see, as humans we tend to portray the person outside different to how we actually feel inside, we wear masks, hollow masks. there may be smiles but they're more to avoid questions than to reflect happiness. and i know they say that the eyes are the windows to the soul, but even they can be deceiving sometimes. we hide our insecurities through elongated laughs and how our voices crack when we're in a middle of a conversation, surrounded by happy people when you're not so happy. we let go off this façade when we're alone, the tears fall from under the smiles we die to hold, our insides crack like glass. we paint pictures of who we aren't for people to see, afraid that the anxiety which clings to us, or the sadness that lives in our eyes will drive them away, scare away anyone of being able to love us. we are shells, walking around pretending to be people and things we are not.

- hollow masks.

breaking

words are too kind
to describe this feeling.

-   how does it feel to break?

breaking

you were my destination
and our love was the map,
i walked on your pathways
got lost in your valleys,
and drowned in your rivers.
sometimes we take a wrong turn,
but with you,
i was in the wrong person.

- pathways.

breaking

depression consumes you
like a shadow that does not know
how to say goodbye.

it's like you're trying to be happy
when people ask you to be happy
but something is pressing on your chest
it takes your hand and it leaves you blinded
and suddenly, you have no control.

no matter how much you want to listen
to everyone and laugh again,
the demons within your mind make it
all feel like a distant dream.

grey clouds are all you see and this
emptiness that consumes you is all
you feel.

- a glimpse of my depression.

breaking

maybe i am just overthinking this like everything else and maybe this is the wrong time to say all the things that make your heart bleed and mine shatter. but sometimes there is no 'right-time' to say things, you just have to clench your jaw, look into their eyes and tell the truth, sometimes you just cannot lie to yourself anymore. so here it goes. our love will not survive, as much as i hate to admit. i had hoped we were the two that escaped the harsh reality that young love does not always last. we are too young to understand, i see my whole world in you, but all i know is that none of us have explored the world yet, we haven't tasted the pain that comes with love and that's why we don't understand.

- the first of many.

breaking

i swear i tried so hard to understand that everything happens for a reason and now i've convinced myself that the reason i am hurting is because the world wants to break me. i am empty, so empty. i am tired, ever so tired. when will this end? i am begging for my sadness to end. i am a ghost walking around, broken inside, i just feel like i do not belong anywhere, i cannot fight anymore. everything is too much. everything is exhausting i am collapsing every day and i am afraid that one-day i will not have any strength to pick myself up.

- i am trying.

breaking

first of all, if you are struggling with suicidal thoughts, please speak to someone, there is help all around it, please seek it, you are special and you will survive, you are a fighter and we all need help. i love you.

there have been many points in my life where i have completely given up, where i have said goodbye to the world, wrote my note and made plans to leave forever. but only twice did i ever go through with it and with god's grace i am here today, thankful, forever grateful. my sadness got to an extent where i could just not fight anymore, i had no strength in my bones to wake up, i could not muster the courage to smile, truth be told i was already half dead, emotionally i was finished, i was just a beating heart waiting to stop. not to go into too much detail but i overdosed twice, two attempts within a week and since then i have not wanted to go back, i was part of the lucky ones who survive to live knowing what it feels like to be on the verge of death. i understood what it felt to wait for death and then realising that this sadness is temporary like everything else in this world, understanding that this pain within me will fade, that this is not the end. i wish i could describe my pain, my mental health and how the universe and everything within it made me want to end my life, but i cannot find words.

suicide is not an option you want to take, it is not something you want no matter how much you convince yourself that it is perfect for you. take it from me, take it from someone who's been there and survived, you are going to be okay. your hardships are going to pass, you are going to grow, the best days of your life are yet to come, hold on.

- suicide.

breaking

and never for a second think that
i have forgotten you.
you helped me stay alive
and so part of you
will always live inside of me.

-    i remember you.

breaking

i have broken so much that
i ended up flirting with death.
i embraced it with both arms
and begged for it to take me.
my chest full of sorrows and my
trembling hands got too much,
the clouds of my past rained on me,
the guilt of tomorrow called,
my problems gave pain to me,
how could i not fall?

- flirting with death.

breaking

my mind is a cage
i cannot escape,
these thoughts hold me
a prisoner,
to a prison i've created.

- prisoner.

breaking

we search for happiness
in the places
it hurts the most.

-    happiness.

breaking

and if i ever get a second chance, i'd pray not to stumble into your soul again. for our eyes never to lock again, for our smiles never to meet again. i wish we had never met and our paths did not cross, maybe everything would be so much better, maybe we should have just stayed strangers. but we fell in love and managed to rekindle the happiness we had lost and then we ended up breaking each other. we were both stuck in the same cycle of searching for love in all the wrong places, in all the wrong people.

-    second chance.

breaking

i met the right person
at the wrong time,
maybe in the next world
you'll be mine.

-     wrong time.

breaking

arms were full of scars
and eyes filled with tears,
i remember looking at the stars,
and seeing all my fears.
the world had given up,
like i had on myself,
for i had given love,
to everything but myself.
sat alone with tears streaming,
hands trembling, heart so cold,
saying please, i must be dreaming,
how could anyone feel so alone?

- scars.

breaking

do you know how it feels to feel like no one in this world loves you? that you force yourself to believe that you are not enough and that you never will be enough. how it feels to be so broken and so sorry for yourself, feeling so empty inside whilst no one really cares, no one asks how you are, do you know what that feels like? it's as though nobody understands you and nobody ever will, that you feel worthless and unappreciated, as though all your efforts go in vain. you feel as though everything will be better off without you, do you know how heart-breaking that feels?

- i thought i will never be enough.

breaking

the thing with suffering from mental health issues is that nobody will ever understand. yes, there are millions of others who suffer with depression, anxiety, bipolar, ocd, eating disorders, the list goes on but the pain you feel is exclusive to you, only you will ever understand it. no matter how much you try to explain to parents or friends, they'll either nod and pretend to understand or diminish your claims that you're suffering, passing it off with another excuse, like you're making excuses not to go to school or you're just simply feeling sad. that hurts. when you know you are completely collapsing but they paint you as a lair, as an attention seeker as though this is a spell you can just break out off, they will never understand how it hugs you, how no matter how hard you try to shake it off, it won't leave. and that just makes it all worse, it makes you feel worse about yourself because nobody understands, nobody *wants* to understand.

- please try to understand me.

breaking

i screamed in pain
and swallowed my guilt,
guilt in finally being happy,
as though i miss the sadness.
that is pain,
believing that you are not
worthy of happiness,
that sadness is your only right.

- pain.

breaking

i swear i knew you, you weren't like this, your eyes did not scream 'with my love comes pain', i could see no danger in your touch so do not blame me for being a fool. your sweet words were so deceiving and so believing so please don't ask me why i did not see this coming. you gave so many promises and every word reassured me that you were the type to stay, the type to give all that i had lost, to remind me of all i had forgot. but in the end, i realised i didn't know you at all.

- people change,
  they become someone we don't know.

breaking

i'm fine
is the biggest lie
to fall from my lips,

i'm fine
means i cry
for a life, not like this.

-      i'm fine.

breaking

lungs full of cigarettes which taste like regret. you see, we search for things to make it easier to forget the people we choose to forget, and we fall in love with these things when we try to forget people we never wanted to forget. the smoke hid my numbness, the way fire found home in my veins and suddenly my lungs could breathe again and though it was toxic, it was something, and to me something was better than nothing. it's crazy how we inhale poison to stay alive, we find what kills us and cling onto it to stay alive. the burnt ashes disappear into the sky the way memories do, the way they light us up and then fade away, how at once they felt so much and now they mean so little.

- cigarettes.

breaking

i guess i took the saying
'it's better to be the one hurting
than the one hurting others'
too seriously because now
i am drowning whilst others
are floating on my happiness.

-      you always meant more.

breaking

the problem is that i care and give too much. there is just something inside of me that makes me want to help and heal everyone, to give parts of myself without thinking about how i'll survive when i'm left empty. i just want the world to be happy and the fact that i cannot assure that makes my heart ache, i've put this self-responsibility upon myself without needing to because that's the type of person i am. my biggest problem is that i want to fix that which is destined to stay broken.

- too much.

breaking

mother why, why can't you see
that this is so much more than sadness.

i am drowning, i am dying.

-    this is me.

write down five of your best memories:

1.)

2.)

3.)

4.)

5.)

reflection

this chapter is about reflection, as you can read from its title. this is a compilation of my thoughts about various aspects of my life, from past relationships, my mistakes, my journey from the breaking and much more. it is me looking back and writing all the lessons and stories i wish i had heard and read, it is me coming clean, almost like a list of confessions. this is me finding closure, in closing the chapter to the past and writing the new. as humans we all make error, but we are defined by how we react to the wrong we do, do we do right or continue to do wrong? i'm a firm believer in forgiving, for if we ask for forgiveness from a higher being then surely, we should forgive those around us, be merciful if you seek mercy. we should stay true to our characters and who we are as people, not falling into what society or the world expects us to be, engage in your uniqueness. sometimes we all should take time and ponder about the past, look at who we were and who we have become. so let's reflect on what there was and what is to be.

reflection

daisies remind me of you,
sweet and delicate.
yet i can crush you
in the sweet palms of my hands,
i can pluck you from all you love.
let me appreciate your beauty,
let me plant our love.

-       daisies.

reflection

forgive me
for being the reason
behind the artwork
on your arms,
you're still a masterpiece.

- artwork.

reflection

i promise i am trying
to do good,
but my good becomes bad,
my intentions are clean,
it makes everyone sad,
i'm not who you've seen.

- we're all trying to change.

reflection

i have shed tears for you
in hope, it will outweigh the
ones which flooded your hope.
you are a broken ship
but i cannot swim.

- sunken.

reflection

mistakes make us human,
mercy makes us strong.

- forgive.

reflection

depression screamed
and sunk its poison into me,
and slowly,
it was all i wanted to feel.

- because sometimes people
  only care for you when you're
  sad.

reflection

being bipolar does not mean
i am happy and i am sad,
i am sad and i am happy.
it means i am a
snowy form in sun filled desserts,
rain without any clouds,
thunder and lightning and then a
gentle breeze.
i am everything.

-    bipolar.

reflection

my happiness came when i finally understood god's reasoning behind my pain. i now bathe in harmony, i read the sweetness of gratitude, i smile at the past.

without breaking you never truly understand what it feels like to be whole. without sadness, you never really know what happiness tastes like. if I did not face the hardest hurdles life has thrown at me, i would not be happy the way i am today.

- when it finally all makes sense.

reflection

first of all, i am sorry. i am sorry for all the hurt i have caused, here i stand with no more excuses, no more sorry's which don't really mean anything, just me with a heartfelt apology. i know i have hurt you and now you face these sleepless nights, where your mind overthinks and the sad songs don't make anything better but i feel them too. the guilt eats me alive but i know it is nothing compared to your sadness. forgive me, forgive me. as humans, we are prone to error, prone to mistakes, i became the person i feared and committed the mistakes i promised myself to stay away from. i promise i never meant to hurt anyone, everything just became a mess and to heal i ended up hurting myself and that resulted in me hurting those around me, i never understood the consequences of my actions. i know that we cannot re-write the past and because of that sometimes i feel hopeless because everything slowly catches up with you, but i believe that everything happens for a reason, that everything has made me stronger and better and i pray the same for you. i hope you find it within your heart somewhere to forgive me, to understand that i am not that person anymore, that i have grown and learnt my lessons.

goodbye, i pray nothing but the best for you.

- apology.

reflection

this is a letter to my past, from here i drop you off at the airport and carry your bags in my trembling hands and i bid you goodbye, forever. i am not entirely proud of our relationship, you and me, we have done a lot of bad but then again, we also did a lot of right, that is why i am the person i am today. to be honest, i owe a lot to you, because of you here i am writing this, here you (the reader) are reading this. i cannot blame you anymore, i can no longer let you control me and affect any future decisions, the bad was my fault and i have grown from it. our relationship was always toxic, we were built on a foundation of a tarnished childhood, mental health problems, the way the world revolves and so much more. you've been good to me too, because of you i looked towards writing, i let the kindness within me drown out everything else but that's made me somebody else, somebody you no longer know. i have made peace with you and everyone else involved so i guess it is time for us to take us separate paths, time for both of us to finally be free and for me to make amends by doing good.

goodbye, thank you for the memories, the good and the bad, you shall soon be forgotten though, for my good will hopefully wipe out the bad.

- to my past.

reflection

you search for identity
in all that is not you.
there will only ever be
one of you,
you are unique and
all you have is yourself,
so find belonging within you.

- unique.

reflection

though a house
may contain a family,
you can't always call it a
home.

- house ain't always a home.

reflection

we forget
that by building others
sometimes
we destroy ourselves.

-     you need someone too.

reflection

we haven't spoken in
god knows how many months,
but still i hope
you remember me.

- please don't forget me.

reflection

i never understood how people move on as though nothing happened, as though the moments we shared never mattered. did those trembles in your spine and tremors in your fingertips when our minds collided mean nothing to you? the way your limbs would freeze and we'd laugh until our stomachs ache, how you could forget all that so easily? i gave you all that made me.

-   was i nothing?

reflection

do not mistake
my kindness as my
ability to accept
all the wrong you do.
i merely forgive,
that's my weakness.

- weaknesses.

reflection

you have planted your ideas
in my soul
and shed seeds in the
palm of my hands.
you have watered the ideas
that cannot escape my lips,
let's pray these roots
hold us together,
because when you love the
way they think,
everything else makes sense.

- growth.

reflection

if you leave,
keep quiet,
leave the keys under the plant, turn off the lights and tip toe quietly down the hallway, do not leave a goodbye note, i don't need to wake up and feel emptier, i'll pretend that you'll come back soon when i cannot find you and do this until i can convince myself that you have gone.

- if you leave.

reflection

one day after you've silently cried into your pillow and hid the scars of the night before under long sleeves in these summer months, take a deep breath and breathe. burn your sins under a hot shower as the sun starts to set and brew yourself a cup of tea or coffee so warm it challenges the sun and fill it with enough sugar to match the love that hides deep inside of you. light that candle you bought ages ago, the one that smells of strawberry and open your windows, let the scent of self-regret and tears leave your room. sip your drink and sit in a blanket, let the candle be your light and have some time to yourself. breathe. lose yourself in a book or movie so good you forget the way it started, find your favourite food and dig through it, i recommend chocolate, you're allowed some on days like these. for one day, just be yourself. for one day just block out all the negativity. no more hiding under a shell of what you think you're supposed to be, just be you. for one day, love yourself. you are a gift to this world.

-    the day after.

reflection

i have come to realise that eventually
everything will be alright. there has
been so many times where i have
believed that i wouldn't make it. that
this is where i'm going to end, that
this is the moment i am going to
break but somehow, we always manage
to pull through. so have faith and
patience, i know things are tough
and hope seems a mile away but the
best things in life come to us when
we least expect it. you're going to be
alright. i promise you it gets better.

- we're all gonna be okay.

reflection

and never for a second believe
that i have forgotten you.
you are the one who showed me
the light when my world was dark,
you are the one who stays alive
in every heartbeat of mine.

i pray your hopes and dreams come true,
i pray you find the happiness that escapes you.
that is the least you deserve.

- i will always remember you
  and all you did for me.

reflection

1.) make a list. write down your goals, what you want to achieve, where you want to be and stick it on a wall. put it somewhere you'd see it every day to remind yourself of where you need to be in life, of what you expect of yourself.

2.) go for walks. walks are amazing, it's just you and your thoughts and nature and it just helps you clear the chaos that lives in your head. the singing of the birds, the brewing breeze, the soft sun, the roaring rain, the sentimental snow, the hard-stone engraved pavements, the gracious grass and purring plants, they just do good to you. get lost and find your way, your intuition is your map.

3.) hold onto people that matter. if people in your life deserve your love and attention and they go good to you, give them your all, love with all your heart and your actions. adorn them with your love and appreciate them. let them know how much they matter.

4.) do what you love. follow your dreams, follow your heart, yes it sounds cliché but find something that makes you happy and stick with it. people will always have an opinion of what you love and do, but it's your life, chase your vision.

5.) be true to yourself. do not change for people, for the world, for friends, for family. stay true to yourself, you are amazing, there is goodness in your heart and great things lie in your destiny.

- five things you need to do.

reflection

i know you want to
hurt yourself,
but every time you do,
it breaks me too.

but sometimes we need to
hurt in order to grow,
so if you need to hurt,
i'll be here with you.

- hurting = road to recovery.

reflection

it is heart-breaking how people, words, emotions and actions cause someone to want to leave everything and everyone, to escape all the care and love and wish to leave this world, to die. we let people out of our grasp, reminding them that they're not worth anything, that the world will go on without them, but no, it won't. every soul contributes to this world revolving, every soul matters equally. we are no better than anyone in terms of our worth, nor are we less. you matter in this world, people will miss you, they will cry and spend nights blaming themselves for your death, you are special, you matter. if no one has ever told you this let me be the first. you do matter. your dreams matter, your aspirations and goals are real, your existence is cherished as much as it feels like it isn't. the best days of your life are yet to come, the people that will appreciate you are going to come, the bad days are going to be left behind and only good will follow you. i know some days everything seems to be collapsing and it feels like you cannot go on anymore, those are the days where your strength is tested, where you are tested and i promise you that you are strong enough to pull through, that you have it within you to fight and you'll soon look back and understand how you fought all your sadness and wonder why you were ever sad in the first place, for the bad times fade and the good times stay.

- listen to me, listen to someone who has
  broke in every way and is grateful for the
  way life has turned out.

reflection

call me at three am and tell me about the bad dream you had and why you can't sleep. if not just call me and absorb the silence, listen to the sounds of our breaths synchronising, i am here for you, i'm here. turn to me and i swear i will care as though our paths never distanced, i know how it feels to need someone but not having anyone, so run to me and i'll give you my undivided attention. swear at me, shout, scream and cry, just let it all out, be angry, be happy, be sad, just be you.

-   always here.

reflection

and as much as it hurts being the nice person and people mistaking your kindness as a weakness, one day you'll find someone who appreciates you for the beautiful soul you are. don't give up being the gentle person who loves too much and gives too much because of a few individuals who never understood your true beauty for you are something special. one day you will change a life, form a smile, make a day and that person will breathe every day because of your kindness, and that's beautiful, right?

-   nice person.

reflection

it hasn't been easy but i've learnt to accept my mental health and all it brings with it. that my depression and anxiety doesn't make me any less, it doesn't make me weak, it doesn't mean i need the pity of others. even with my personality disorder, as horrible as it sounds, it's part of me, it gives me the love i have and the sadness that breaks me. all i am gifted with is because i am capable of facing it, yes, it is a gift despite the problems because everything happens as a blessing. with time people will accept you and your mental health too, and with time you'll learn to live with and accept it. let it in, it exists within you, it is part of you but it won't defeat you. with love and support, from yourself and others, with help and guidance, with prayer and the universe, you'll learn to tame it.

- acceptance.

reflection

and if i see you happy
with someone else,
smile at me so i can
smile at you too,
glad that we shared something
not sad that it is lost.

  -   love what you had,
      do not grieve what is gone.

reflection

though the scars may never fade,
the lessons we lean shall forever be
imprinted on our hearts,
the blade may pierce our skin
but it will never damage our
determination to keep fighting.
blood may pour,
but hope will never vanish.

- long sleeves.

reflection

sometimes it's just hard to get over certain things in life, be it the death of a loved one, a close friend leaving or just personal problems you may be facing. they leave us without sleep, forever wondering about the countless possibilities and regrets on how maybe we could've done things better. we live in this bubble of 'what if', lost in thoughts of the past, unable to find the answer destiny has written. you're allowed to be sad, you can mourn and cry and drown yourself in early 2000's sad songs, that is your right, nobody said you're not allowed to feel your sadness and engage in it. but then you need to think about what it all means. everything within this universe has a story behind why it's happening, and maybe this sadness which is temporary will help you in the long term. maybe it'll inspire something new or bring someone new, there is always good on the other side.

- a lesson i've learnt.

reflection

there are going to be some days where you won't be able to open your eyes in the morning for school, college, uni, work, whatever it may be, either because your worries kept you up till five am or you've been crying so much your eyes have started to swell. these days are tiring, i know, these are the days you're going to want to go back to sleep and never wake up, to hide under your duvet and shut yourself from the world. but remember that these days will come and go, these days are the days where the world will fight against you and you're going to win. so get up, brush your teeth, wash your face and wipe your eyes, put on something you love and keep faith that you're going to get through the day, because you will.

- for the bad days.

reflection

we worry so much
about all that could
go wrong,
we forget to look around
and appreciate all that
went right.

- look around, there is goodness around you.

take five minutes to ponder about life
and then write a letter to the future you
to read in six months:

recovery

this chapter is about recovery, about using both the breaking and the reflection to rebuild yourself, to heal, to regroup all the broken puzzles of your soul that have scattered. i include the idea of self-love and how as humans we complete ourselves, not destroying the idea of love but merely putting a different perspective to it. also, i speak about coping with mental health issues, learning to pick yourself up and just generally more good feeling poetry. whatever happens to us, at the end we will recover. you see life is a combination of ups and down, good days and bad days. so when you go down you're bound to come up, and you'll go down again yes but that's to learn another lesson and then you're right back up again. recovering isn't easy, it's so much easier to say than do, it takes time, several setbacks, days where you isolate yourself with your thoughts but we pull through, we manage to cross the finishing line with a smile on our faces. several things help aid your recovery and i guess you'll just have to continue reading to find out.

recovery

as humans,
we complete ourselves.
we were born as an
entire puzzle,
we find the missing pieces
from within,
not from others.

-    you're already complete, you just need
     to put the pieces together.

recovery

it was not that
i did not understand your love,
and you didn't understand mine.
it was that,
you failed to understand
i loved you the way
you deserved to be loved,
too much.
and that is where i went wrong.

- it's not always your fault,
  sometimes they just won't
  ever understand.

recovery

freedom meant
unshackling myself
from the demons of
the past that
hugged me goodnight.

- freedom for the soul.

recovery

at the end
of each passing day,
you're the only one
guaranteed to stay.

so please do not
glve all your love away,
for even you need some
during those lonely nights you lay.

- only you deserve so much love.

recovery

pain
was the only teacher
that taught me
you don't have to
understand what i teach,
just learn to embrace
all that i give with
welcoming arms.

they say a guest is a gift,
your pain is a guest in
the flowerbed of your chest,
give it a home and watch it
leave.

- lessons.

recovery

time is the medicine
we ache for.
but we don't know
where it grows.

- time is precious.

recovery

i wish i had believed them
when they had said
you'll be okay.
because now i feel like
a butterfly bursting out
its cocoon to fly away,
revival.

- belief.

recovery

i find solace
in the fact
that maybe others
understand the
chaos which
dances inside my
chest,
we are together.

- others understand too.

recovery

better days
lie on the horizon,
keep swimming.
don't let yourself drown yet.

-      my words are your lifeguard.

recovery

you come to realise that someone has more scars, more reasons to not wake up and despite your heart aching in your chest, you have one. you have eyes that tear and hands that tremble and despite them giving you panic attacks at three am when the world dies in its sleep, some don't even have that privilege, of a roof to hide their attacks, of long sleeves to cover a nights worth of painting your body in heartbreak.

your pain does matter, it matters as much as the earth matters to us, everything.

but for a moment, appreciate all that you have rather than all you've lost, and for a fraction of a second you might just feel better.

-   blessings help us heal,
    they are everywhere.

recovery

friendship was the best
medicine i overdosed on,
but we forget that an
overdose of anything
always leads to destruction.
be careful of who you let in.

- broken friendship.

recovery

if someone claims to
be your friend
but all they give you
is everlasting hurt,
that is unnecessary baggage.
don't weigh yourself down
feeding on their words,
don't let them stop you flying.

- leave bad friends at the airport
  and fly away.

recovery

my childhood was spent smiling
because i wanted to smile.
so why did we grow up
and complicate everything?

stop searching for reasons
behind the simple things in life.
and just like the child you,
just do, what makes you, you.

- growing up.

recovery

we bleed
for the love we need.
we feel
the wrong things to heal.
we search
only to find hurt.
so let go
of all you know.
stop complicating,
less finding more creating.
you see
if it's meant to be.
this earth
gave it to you at birth.
and when
the time is right it'll be sent.
you are
a journey so far.
so strap up,
your seatbelt love.
let's ride
the road of life.
let's break
and learn to ache.
let's hurt
to understand our worth.
let's fall
to find our all.

-    everything.

recovery

your pain is a combination of all that has happened to you in life and all that shall happen, truth is, it won't stop. pain in life never leaves, it's like a family member who doesn't realise they've overstayed their visit, and when they finally go back to their own homes they're back two weeks later. life is full of good days and bad days, ups and downs, pain and happiness. you have to understand that one day you'll stop feeling the pain and you'll taste the happiness which hides underneath those crescent moon smiles you fake. it will taste like honey and you wouldn't want to stop tasting. but your pain will come back in a different form, a different selection of words and emotions but what keeps you going is knowing that soon you'll taste your happiness again. as your pain increases, so does your happiness. you cannot escape pain, you learn to accept it, to give it a home and then let it find its way out until it comes back again seeking shelter. have belief, if you want to survive you have to believe you can. your pain is a lesson and your worries are the exam, you're going to ace both and find peace, your reward.

- pain, in its simplest explanation.

recovery

we have a choice
to either drown in
our sadness and
let it suffocate us
till we gasp for air

or

we can make amends
for the wrong we have
done and forgive the
wrong done to us

we

create our own destiny,
write our own serenity,
fix our own mistakes,
live our own lives.

-     the choice is yours.

recovery

time heals everything.
we are so worried
and concerned with
rushing all in life,
we forget that time
heals what actions
and words cannot.
take a step back,
take a deep breath.

- *sabr* my friend.

recovery

recovery means
waking up one day
and not feeling the best,
but that feeling of not
wanting to wake up
at all doesn't haunt
your mind as much as
it did before.

it is slow,
but keep going.

> \- slow steps,
>   rest your hurt head.

recovery

recovery means
seeing what once broke you
and not letting their words
drown you.
their words bounce off your
skin for galaxies beam within
and your heart has finally
found peace.

- this is how you know.

recovery

we try to save everyone
except ourselves,
even the best of us
need some help.

- save you more than
  anyone else.

recovery

my mother holds enough love
to be a father too,
it shows that a woman is
strong enough to break and
build, to ache and heal.
you learn what importance
the role of a father holds,
but how a mother's love
paves over those holes.
her smile has sacrificed
everything and more for me,
so how could i mourn his
absence in such misery.

-     my entire world.

recovery

being happy does not mean
you do not have issues,
it just means you are working
hard on trying to fix them.

-    what happiness is.

recovery

there is goodness in your heart
and kindness in your words,
hold onto these,
it's all you need.

- keep your heart soft.

recovery

the reason you are suffering is because you haven't learnt to forgive yourself, you keep blaming yourself for everything that went wrong and everything that could go wrong. that is why emptiness fills you. you are human you are bound to do wrong so have mercy on yourself, you're doing good. sometimes things are out of our control and we can do nothing but watch the chaos unfold. it's the hardest thing to do, forgiving yourself, because holding yourself to blame makes everything make more sense but slowly it's breaking you, it's creeping in your every decision and those late nights where your brain decides to hurt you. the best of us are those who are merciful, so be merciful to the person you met first in this world and the person you'll meet last, yourself.

- forgive yourself.

recovery

i wish i could say,

i hate you, i hate you, i hate you for making me believe that i was not worthy of any form of love, that my hands are flawed and that they destroy everything they touch. you left me and i was sat there convincing myself that everything is wrong with me, you let my insecurities strangle me but no, you were the problem. you drowned me in an everlasting cycle of self-hate and self-destruction to an extent i didn't recognise myself anymore and for that i hate you.

but i can't,
and maybe that is recovery,
that my love
surpasses my hate,
that i forgive with my all.

- mature.

recovery

in your chest you feel this tightness,
you imagine lying ever so lifeless.
all you think about is leaving,
to give up and stop breathing.
you start to resort to self-harm,
plagued with scars across your arms.
the pressure of life gets too much,
everything just becomes too tough.
and it feels like this is enough,
how can you live so void of love?
every passing day means hope fades,
you forget memories, nothing feels the same.
all around you are blurred faces and souls,
feeling so empty, so far from whole.
thoughts leave you trapped, you can't escape,
hurt heart and shattered faith.
let me tell you it does get better,
take my hand, we'll face it together.
i promise you you're not alone,
there's support in and out of home.
the clouds will move for the sky,
your problems will do the same for life.
what seems to end your today,
will tomorrow die away.
so please for one more day,
with me here please do stay.
you'll be free of the fire in your chest,
you're gonna survive and pass this test.

- surviving suicide.

recovery

when they say you've got six months to live it means you've got six months to love everything your heart has been afraid to love. it means you've got six months to convince yourself that your dreams are not merely dreams but realities you never understood, or dared to understand. it means you've got six months to decode the mystery of the earth before it swallows you. it means you've got six months to grab each of the eighty-six thousand four hundred seconds within the day, and for every second you miss you weep for time makes gold look like wood. it means you've got six months, but who knows if we've even got tomorrow.

- the clock continues to click.

recovery

despite everything
and all the breaking,
we always manage
to come out better
and stronger people.
we always find a way
to pull through.

- you're gonna pull through.

put a photo of someone you love here, so you always remember them.

the world

this chapter and the following ones are a little less person to my life, they are more general whilst still being personal to my beliefs and thoughts. this chapter covers the world, what this *dunya* is meant to give to us, what it actually gives to us, and the widespread problems that pollute it. ranging from racism to world peace, human characteristics to war, masculinity to femininity, different topics discussed within society. it goes a bit deeper into education and corruption within governments, all that juicy stuff. (don't worry it's not all covered in this chapter, there's other topics in the 'overthinking' chapter and the 'the reader' chapter). we all know this beloved earth of ours is slowly falling, we are losing faith in humanity but i aspire for my words to spark some inspiration, to educate and to ignite a burning desire within you to better it. we are the new generation, it's our job to make sure things are done correctly, that we learn from the mistakes, problems and atrocities of our predecessors.

the world

this world my dear,
it is designed to bring
you down to your knees.
its philosophy is heartbreak,
and you cure for it
is mercy.

- forgive and forgive again.

the world

we use violence
to preach the
message of
stopping violence,
it's an endless
cycle we cannot
escape.

-     violence.

the world

it is so sad to see how material
goods hold much more
importance than human lives,
almost as though poverty and
slavery were not the faults of
man, as though it wasn't the same
before but oh how they banish
history from their guilt and blame
us.

- you started the problem and
  then you pretend it doesn't
  exist.

the world

world peace seems
a world away,
but the first step
is kindness.
be kind to your
neighbour and
they will
be kind to the world.

-       the first step is kindness
        to you and around you.

the world

social justice is blind, dumb and deaf, as though if you're coloured you're stamped guilty and given death. the system is corrupted but still isn't being interrupted, hearing stories online but not from the media, no more propaganda lies, no more coloured lies as though its sepia. only listen to the people that have tasted the evil, that have lived the tough and embraced the rough, videos retweeted and tensions heated, just waiting for the oppressors to be defeated. pleads are ignored as the officer's scream for more, hands raised but he's trapped in, no offences except for his coloured skin. that's another innocent murdered, more whispers murmured, media reports he was a threat but now a man who has done nothing is dead. where is the justice? this isn't once or twice, this has happened over a thousand times, we've lost a thousand lives, coloured justice isn't something that only exists today, it's been going on for centuries once colonisation took its place. and now there is silence because a coloured person is immune to laws against violence, and yes i may not share the same skin nor can i begin to imagine what they're fighting, but i share the same heart of oppression and that's why i'm writing.

-    coloured justice.

the world

i hate how it feels as though
this world has given up on
this generation of mine.

how can we progress when
the sins of the generation
above keep raining on us?
we are labelled with
brokenness yet you broke us,
so, don't refer to the advice
you throw down our necks,
refer to your wrongs which
infect our every right.

- inherited sins.

the world

the poor
are the richest
of us all,
for they have
no addiction
to this world.

- poor, but rich inside.

the world

for this world, our world.

times are tough and fear has made its mark, but we have to keep faith in our hearts. we are made of resilience, strength and unity, we stand against all types of wrong through our diversity. the world wants us to hate and keep on hating, but we've woken up so tell them to keep on waiting. powerful people want us to turn on one another, so let us stand united as sisters and brothers. we are not defined by the riches we hold or how we fall to sin, neither the religion we follow or the colour of our skin. we are defined by the character we are and the goodness inside, whether or not we try to do good in this life. our world is slowly crumbling so listen to my one request, the power lies in the hands of the people so please never forget. rather than turning and pushing the blame, we should look at how we're all the same, rather than pointing fingers and attacking our own, let's try and heal our home.

- our world.

the world

my religion of peace is
exploited on the tv.
and now the actions of a few
hold the majority view.
they don't take time to listen
about the beauty of my religion.
they want to take things out of context
as politicians scream out nonsense.
they are using violence against us
and then say they don't mean to offend us.
their retaliation is so much worse
as it leaves us innocent and so hurt.
and now my women walk in fear
of being attacked for what they wear.
my men are seen as alien to society
as we absorb hate with a smile so silently.
my religion is of peace, love and freedom,
of mercy, family and healing.
so don't paint us with what you read,
paint us with what you see.

- islamophobia.

the world

i'm tired of pretending that racism doesn't exist, i'm tired of bombings, hate and shit. i'm tired of these songs dominating the charts, distracting people from the bombs in iraq. i'm tired of double standards and hypocrisy, no equality for you and me. i'm tired that we're ignoring children and women dying, tired that we turn a blind eye to the millions crying. tired that we label refuges as migrants, tired of all this silence. i hate that the colour of my skin and my religion mean my words aren't worthy to listen. tired of insanity and lost humanity. how the government tells us that we're fine but we're still riddles with hate crime. education is a right but it's denied on purpose, they don't want to teach us why they hurt us. the world is breaking and i'm tired, equal justice is all that's desired. i'm tired that a muslim is called a terrorist, but a white person is called mentally ill like they don't know what terror is. i'm tired at how girls still get killed before they enter the world. it's as though the rules only apply to some of us, that promises break as soon as politicians won our love. there's so many double standards it doesn't make sense, but the leaders still sit back like nothing is wrong and pretend.

-     i'm tired.

the world

they say a man has
to be strong,
but strength is measured
in muscles and anger,
assertion and fame.
not in fighting every
mental battle within,
kindness and empathy,
choosing good over bad.
and that's where we
go wrong.

- man.

the world

being a male makes it harder to release your emotions because we are seen as species that conceal their feelings inside and once we do open up we are easily judged. we are labelled as soft, weak and vulnerable, as though we aren't allowed to feel, cry or break. it makes everything hard, as though we don't have a right and we have to uphold this guard of strength and masculinity, this mask that we cannot take off. and what that does is force us bottle everything inside, to slowly break until our chest explodes like a volcano and we completely fall until we cannot put ourselves together again.

-   man's emotions.

the world

women
are the backbone
to society,
the anchor which
keeps us afloat,
a lighthouse of
hope.

-    cherish them.

the world

she said,

boys cannot cy
for their tears are dry
you can ask me why.

i asked,
they hide their feelings in roof top ceilings,
the smoke they inhale
and the looks they entail.
they are afraid you see
of this thing called society,
who don't accept it
but neither do they reject it.
so boys don't cry
and instead they lie
on their beds
with chaos in their heads.
because the world said no,
and that's how it goes.

-       boys cannot cry.

the world

my mother once said that women are strong,
i asked why
for i always saw her cry
and surely tears
mean you've broken to your fears.

she said,
her heart is wide enough to hold her worries and the worries of a man,
her smile is warm enough to ease the gentle cries of a child. her touch
brings a man weak in his knees, her innocence softens the harshness
within the heart of a father. her silence is the most beautiful song, she
cries, but so does everyone else, but not everyone else holds the burdens
of a family on the curve of their backs. her feet encompass heavens, and
her speech is soft like the clouds. her hands possess threads which build
homes out of houses and smiles out of broken hearts. women are strong,
strong in ways one cannot imagine.

i was silenced.

-   what i learnt as a male.

the world

we are constantly told that
humanity has disappeared,
but that is because we
search for it where it never
existed, government.

- house of horror.

the world

my gun is this pen,
my blood is the ink,
let's win the war within.

- gunshots.

the world

the lands of my people
will soon blossom,
full of roses and
snow-capped mountains,
liberation of women,
and the sweet laughter
of children that will light
up the barren streets.
oh how i ache for peace.

- home is where my heart lives.

the world

oh blessed land where dates
once bloomed, and the sun
would hide in shyness.
your time will come,
your tide would run
to kiss the shore awake.

- palestine.

the world

young child who flees wars
my words cannot describe,
your smile bears pain
my nation cannot imagine.
there is this courage to you
that a thousand men cannot break,
your resilience is my strength,
come find home in our hearts.

-   war child.

the world

we mistake
peace and freedom
for being the same.
peace doesn't mean freedom,
nor does freedom mean peace.

- peace and freedom aren't
  the same.

the world

you escape your home
in search for one in
earth's heart,
but humanity turned its back,
it told the sea to drown
you, it told you come to our
houses but we won't let you
in. and then it wipes the guilt
away, by saying in death you
should have stayed, why did
you have to come all this
way? if only they knew the
pain your eyes have seen,
if only they knew what it
felt to bleed.

- migrant.

the world

you could've saved many lives, you could've been a doctor if you were alive. you could've made your younger sister smile, you could've made your mother proud at five. your life was stolen and now your hope is broken, your families heart is left open as they hold onto moments. they were hoping but now they're barely coping, your killers are joking, your legacy they're smoking, your death to them was a token, a truth left so unspoken. you weren't just a refugee, you were just like me, you breathed humanity but were killed by insanity, you faced such brutality whilst you lived rationally. you were killed by corrupt politicians, left in an empty position, you had so much ambition, you dreamed of a school admission, you were travelling to a new mission, but now you're gone and fake apologies you're forced to listen.

- to you migrant child,
  aylan kurdi, washed
  up on the shore.

the world

if she wants to cover her hair and her body, let her, what difference does it make to you? she's stood in silence minding her own business so what right do you hold to object? she's doing what makes her happy, what gives her peace, that is her human right. how dare you? how dare you try and take that right away?

- you do you.

the world

war was never the solution,
it was the direct result of evolution,
evolution of society and revolution,
revolution of the rich's contribution,
they take more with less distribution,
do less with more retribution,
dividing the united and creating pollution,
leading to more innocent persecution,
and then to find a resolution,
they invest in more institution,
and the victim is society,
we've lost the morals of humanity,
trapped in a calamity,
of this insanities reality,
but then they get mad at me,
for wanting peace, not brutality,
blame the innocent, it's so sad to see,
seeing the helpless lying to bleed,
it is unity we need,
for the oppressed to finally be freed,
but we're obsessed with greed,
our desires are all we ache to feed.

- war is made by man,
  but the world holds
  the blame.

the world

when you are declaring war
against children in the street
and widowed mothers, against
broken sticks, rocks and
endless cries.
this is not war,
it is your genocide.

- genocide.

the world

we are taught history
and all the wrong that
was done.
but we do the same,
if not worse, for our
wars to be won.

- we're the same
  as our so called
  enemies.

the world

we are trapped in this stigma of wanting war, this everlasting desire to want more. but don't you understand we are tired and sore, tired of death and seeing bodies on the floor. there's leaders taking power so sure, but they're ignoring broken families at the door. is this the future you want to draw? are these the memories you want them to store? you leave them broken from the horror they saw, tears streaming, broken to the core. where is the freedom? where is the law? you didn't help, and now bodies lay by the shore.

- war-torn refugees.

the world

you take their innocence
with every gasping breath,
muffled screams and squirming hands,
as they plead for death.
and now they live
with permanent fear,
dead whilst living,
breaking with every tear.

- rape.
  it is not your fault.

the world

i wonder how the world would be
when peace and love is all we see.

i wonder how the world would be,
where happiness is our priority.

i wonder how the world would be,
where our dreams are never lonely.

i wonder how the world would be,
where our freedom is free.

i wonder how the world would be,
when war doesn't surround me.

i wonder how the world would be.

- i wonder.

write down three ways you can make the world a better place:

1.)

2.)

3.)

the reader

this chapter is not so personal yet personal at the same time, it is more towards you, the reader. this poetry mainly consists of advice pieces, poetry which makes you feel better about yourself, poetry which makes sense of that chaos within your head that you don't really understand. some of these will hit you deep, others may not hit a nerve, it depends on what you've been through and how much you can relate, most of these are relatable to me. but it is not me here complaining and making poetry of my pain, no, that is within the previous chapters, here i try and make lessons out of them, i try and find healing within the pain, nectar within the poison if i must say. so draw wisdom from this chapter, find the answers to the questions that keep you awake at night.

the reader

you believe the scars you wear
shall never disappear.
and sometimes they don't,
or maybe they won't,
for it is a reminder of all
the battles you have faced
and defeated.
a sign of your survival,
embrace them,
they are your war wounds.

- scars.

the reader

you are beautiful
in all your uniqueness,
be proud of who you are,
of what you are.

    god crafted your beauty,
    and he makes no mistake.

the reader

you sometimes have to let go off people whilst not completely understanding why yourself, for the pain of holding on will scar you, it will break you. in life we are going to have to leave people for the best, either for your good or for their good, for holding onto that rope burns your hand, you do more bad than good if you force something that isn't meant to be. we're bound to lose people, either we let go or they let go and it does kill, a lot, but believe in destiny. faith is your companion, so hold onto it for better things will come into your life, better people will come. i guess you don't really lose anyone, because better people come and replace them, people who prove their worth, people who make you feel better than before. everything happens for its own beautiful reason, we lose to gain, we hurt to grow.

- letting go.

the reader

you want to
heal the world.
but what about
the chaos
inside of you?

>   you matter as much as the
>   world because you come
>   from it.

the reader

you hurt because you
sprinkle poison onto
the tongues of the
ones you love and
then let them strangle
you with their words.

- sweet words become toxic.

the reader

you have to look in the mirror
and love what you see,
for i promise that someone
will see so much more.
you are beautiful.

- your flaws won't seem
  like flaws anymore.

the reader

maybe you will meet them
again, when you're wiser
and life is a little less chaos.

maybe you were the wrong
people at the right time
but when you became the
right people it was the
wrong time.

maybe you were just never
meant to be written, or
maybe your chapters will
cross paths again to form
a story.

have faith in what life gives.

-   what is meant to be,
    will always be.

the reader

you search for
happiness in
where you had
once lost it.

the world doesn't
work like that,
stop running to
what hurt you
in hope of a
different ending.

- you wish for everything
  to be different, but it won't.

the reader

you paint
your sad eyes
on a happy face.

no wonder you're
breaking, embrace
your sadness, for
it is the strongest
part of you.

- it's okay to be sad.

the reader

the ocean was born with drowning in her lungs, she doesn't mean to but it is all she knows. pain was born but it held love, yet her innocent hands only ever felt hate and so her waves crash and her horizon runs in fear, no wonder you can never catch it. she doesn't mean to hurt, that is why she leaves.

- sometimes people only cause pain
  because it's all they've felt.

the reader

i am sorry and i know right now this doesn't sound so poetic and there aren't any rhymes nor fancy metaphors, these words probably don't even make sense and my grammar is awful. i hate early mornings and when my tea gets cold or how signs to where you live bring back so much but i just really wanted to tell you one thing but i don't know how to say it or if you'll say the same back. i really don't know, i'm just overthinking everything but, i miss you. i really do.

- sometimes the least words
  mean the most.

the reader

you
knew how to
love me when
i was sad.

- irony.

the reader

you
give and give
until you are
left empty.
if only
someone did
the same for
you.

- empty.

the reader

you staple yourself
to memories and
let them replay.
and yet you wonder
why you cannot
seem to forget.
accept and let go,
burn who you were,
paint who you are.

- new beginnings.

the reader

you tell me
your sadness does not end.
but do you really want it?

do you do good to others?
as you would for yourself?

do you wake up at dawn?
and whisper silent prayers?

do you only focus on the bad?
and forget the good?

do you try and find the wisdom
behind your hurt?

do you?

- search.

the reader

you hold
your own
world in
your own
hands.
don't let
anyone
else write
your story.
be the
best
author.

- yours.

the reader

1.) tell the truth despite the consequence
2.) give your mum lots of compliments
3.) take a breath and absorb the moment
4.) remember we heal after we're broken
5.) breathe in the cold fresh air
6.) understand it's okay to have fear
7.) spend nights laughing with friends
8.) be who you are, no need to pretend
9.) draw, sing, write, dance, scream, just express
10.) always, please always, try your best

- ten tips to enjoy life.

the reader

good things come with patience. you cannot rush things that are meant to be, you cannot force things to happen when they aren't destined to happen. you just have to wait with faith, hold hope in your heart and a smile on your face on both the good days and the bad days for they'll both lead you to your destination. every little thing isn't so little, the smallest things make the biggest differences and they all happen for a reason. you just have to find that reason rather than bringing yourself down as often we forget that hurt is the direct route to healing, that disappointment leads you to success, if what you want doesn't happen, understand something better is on its way, always stay hopeful my friend.

- patience.

the reader

1.) look at the moon and admire it as though you have never seen it before.
2.) tell someone they're beautiful and admire the changes within their face.
3.) don't drink coffee for a week and then sit down and have a double expresso, feel the drug surge through your veins.
4.) call an old friend.
5.) put your phone away and for a night, capture memories through your mind, not snapchat.

- five things you must do.

the reader

you need good friends,
people who make you
smile on the days you
can't.
people with whom you
can laugh until your
ribs ache.
people with whom you
can create a truckload
of memories with.
good friends build a
good life.

- friendship.

the reader

there is more to life than them. there are cafes that serve steaming hot caramel latte's with cosy sofas in the corner and picturesque artwork from spain on the wall. it has waiters that smile at you and the feel of home. there are shop window with displays and children laughing as they chase their younger siblings down the road with their mother hurrying behind. there are rainy wednesday mornings when the patter of rain hits your roof and wakes you up and calm sundays where you feel like the world is in your hands. there are conversations at four am with close friends in cars with good playlists that go on for hours as the stars smile down at you, conversation so deep the lyrics within the song fade in shyness. there are clean sheets and lemon smelling rooms waiting for you when you come back from a long day of work, there is the excitement of waiting for the next day. there are adventures in other countries, foods to be tasted, walks in the parks and holding the hand of someone who won't let go. there is so much more to heartbreak.

- there is a world out there,
  greater than that one person.

the reader

to the pain that lives within you, hush it with a finger on her lips. tell her to keep the noise down because tomorrow is a school night and at seven thirty am you are going to have to break the heart of your bed and wish it goodbye. ask it to whisper and tip-toe down the hallways of your mind, ask it to take a seat because you need time to think without your hands trembling or your leg shaking without you realising. you want to imagine fields of burnt yellow tulips, scarred from the sun and grass so green the cows are afraid to chew it. like the movies, like the movies, like the movies. maybe not everything has a happy ending but who said we believed in endings? tell your pain to lower her voice because you have survived wars you cannot describe. ask your pain to grab an umbrella in case it rains and to tie its laces so it doesn't trip. ask and ask for the pain lives within you and you own it.

-   the pain within you.

the reader

as humans, we wish to slow down time to enjoy the good in life and speed up time to rush through the hardships. how we wish as humans to go back in time to re-live the good days and go forward in time to the so believed better days. we, as people, we are always in conflict, we want this or we want that, we are lost in our emotions and we are drowning in our thoughts. we wish to slow time because we forget to appreciate the good moments when we have them, we're either lost in the constant intoxication of the past or we're too afraid of our happiness slipping that we forget to live it. we wish to speed up time not understanding that it is the hardships that make us who we are, the difficult moments in life are what make us strong. so remember to live before you aren't living so much anymore. appreciate the moments in your life now before they're gone. to speed up time, hope. to slow down time, love.

-    time.

the reader

cancer
comes and wraps its arms around you, like a distant family member you only see during the holidays, unfamiliar. you try and recognise them through the sound of their voice, or the hollow echoes of their rhythmic footsteps, but it feels like a stranger. it strangles you, rolls a dice on your life, pulls out a deck of cards that hasn't been shuffled, a paper full of cheat codes, everything against your favour. your body becomes a board game, you hope for luck, you pray for victory, you are a survivor or the greatest battles your body has seen, you are fighting the entire universe.

- cancer.

the reader

sometimes cancer comes and takes away the people that you love the most, this deadly disease that slowly snatches life, pulling it out like a loose thread. to the ones we've lost, we salute your fight, your courage, your passion. as much as we wanted to stop it, to take our bare hands and pull it out, to grab it by the collar and scream, 'why are you torturing my family', we can't. and so agony sets in the ceilings of our hearts but contentment lies on the ground. we remember them leaving as fighters, stronger than we'll ever be.

- we'll pray for you.

write a letter to the past, what would you have told your past self?

spirituality

this chapter is about the concept of spirituality, both in terms of religion and peace within one's self. as a muslim, religion is a big part of me, my faith stems from god, i guess religion holds a foundation within me upon which everything else grows. on my darkest of days religion has saved me, on my best of days religion has only made me happier. i understand not everyone believes in a religion, maybe you believe but not in a god, we're all different, but whatever you believe in, keep faith within it. find your inner peace. meditate. go for a walk. talk to a friend. we're humans, not robots, we all need a break, a retreat, someone to release too, we need to relax sometimes. take ten minutes to yourself every morning to ponder, where are you in life, where have you been, and where do you want to go. continue to better yourself.

spirituality

i pray god grows roses where once
only thorns grew. that peace fills
the emptiness within your heart
and love fills the cracks within your
soul. that the sadness within you
becomes contentment and finally
that my prayers are accepted.

- i pray for your wellbeing.

spirituality

the words of my lord
unlocked the shackles
which tied my heart
to sadness.
his mercy set me free.

-     mercy.

spirituality

i searched for a hand to hold
and a heart to listen,
forgetting that the one who
created me understood me
the most.

- you were always there.

spirituality

i was lost and then you
guided me, because the
love of this world has
blinded me.

your love and your kindness
saved me, the peace of your
message and your mercy
made me.

- you found me.

spirituality

for me, religion is a major part of my life, it is the foundation for my living, my map in this world to guide me to where i am meant to be. as a muslim, god's words of mercy and love, his message of good character and a clean heart speak to me, the way of life ordained by him is the one that gives me happiness, a kind of happiness which nothing else could give me. my heart feels content and at ease whilst praying. i place my faith in god and his written destiny, believing in his plan for me, and how he loves me and wants the best for me. he is there for me to speak to, vent to, cry and beg to and the fact that after disobeying him he still grants us blessings, shows his mercy and love. religion gives me a purpose, a belonging.

- what religion means to me.

spirituality

thank you, god, for your countless
blessings that not even a lifetime
of pondering could cover. you
have given me everything, both
your good and bad, blessings and
tests bring me to today. and i
wouldn't have it any other way.

- forever grateful.

spirituality

this world
is temporary.
our happiness
lies in the next.

-       hereafter.

spirituality

i was told about a man whose smile shined
like the moon when the night sky of sadness
fell upon him, a man who wept for me
centuries before i was born.

- may peace and blessings be upon you.

spirituality

you need to find peace within yourself before you decide to seek peace within the world. you need to make peace with yourself before you try and make peace with others. you ask, how do you find and make peace? you forgive, both yourself and others. you learn to be kind to your tired soul, accepting that you will have faults and days where you don't feel like yourself. you take care of yourself mentally and emotionally by putting yourself first when you need to. find peace within the little things that mean the most, within loved ones and hobbies. be easy on your soul, it has been through so many troubles and drowned in so many oceans of sadness. it is a gradual process to becoming a better person, take a deep breath, you're on a journey.

- finding peace.

spirituality

you have to fall in
love with your own
company,
for you are the most
important person in
your life,
you deserve some time
for you.

- solitude.

spirituality

you need to take a walk
with no destination and
let the wind guide you.
find yourself sat at small
coffee shops on street
corners, find yourself
lost in your thoughts, the
way the clouds become
lost within each other.
inhale the fresh air and
take a moment to plan
your next step.

-    life's plan.

spirituality

1.) take 15 minutes out of your day to reflect, meditate, pray, for a few minutes just detach yourself from the world, 15 out of 1440.
2.) belief. not necessarily in a higher being or entity, but in yourself, that you will rekindle the good parts of you.
3.) co-existence. understand that not everyone will share the same belief as you, respect that, teach one another, live peacefully in your differences.
4.) read. read loads of books on loads of things. read about the past, the present, the future, you, me, this, anything. words make sense of thoughts.

- four ways to develop your spirituality.

spirituality

take a deep breath,
feel the air surging
within you.
you are alive.
that is the greatest
blessing of them all.

- life.

<u>write down a prayer for you and your loved ones:</u>

for the culture

this chapter is the shortest chapter in the back, it's inspired by a phrase i've always seen on twitter, for the culture. this is just an amalgamation of poems reflecting my pakistani culture, quite similar to other south asian cultures. moreover, there are poems reflecting unity, how culture doesn't divide us, how we are one as humans. i love my culture but i don't let it define me, i don't put the mask of nationality upon myself, i see myself as a child of the earth, we're different yet we're all the same.

for the culture

you adorn thick cotton
made by stronger hands,
colours rich like spices,
colours soft like the sky.
your fragrance entices me,
samosas being friend,
fresh oil set on the side,
the sweet language of home.
how urdu lies on the tongue,
punjabi; pashto; pothwari,
i wish i could express my love
in every one
of those beloved languages.
you are the smiles of the elderly,
full of stories captured in
their rich soil brown eyes,
brown like the kameez's,
we wear to mosques,
and to the temples,
yet so much pure.
you are home,
my smile lies in your valleys,
my hope in your mountains.
my freedom in your people,
your love within me.

- homeland.

for the culture

the women of my land wear bangles as thick as the curve of the moon, clinging together in a melody of happiness. veils dressed gently upon their fragile heads and shy smiles, beauty lies in their hands, how they are so gifted by its beholder. they are strong in heart, ferocious in courage, all which remaining soft, like the *chapatis* they make, sweet like the *ladoos* they enjoin. the women of my land have thick arched eyebrows and heavy hands, but i have not seen any more precious.

-    women of my land.

for the culture

we share different homes,
different cultures and
different colours of our skin.

but we are all the same within.

-    you and i are the same.

for the culture

my heart lies in rich roads coloured with spices,
fields spreading over acres but its love captured
within a grain of rice. beeping taxis, shalwar
kameez's, mango lassi, samosas on the streets,
the call for prayer blaring, the shaking of hands
in peace, coloured scarves, slippers which clap
the warm marble floor, kids playing cricket in
the middle of the road, bazaars, bargaining
aunties, warm sunsets, biryani,
love and compassion, a home at every opening
door.

-   i miss home.

for the culture

eid brings lanterns lit
and hung outside the
doors of our homes.
the sweet laughter of
children that is nectar
to the ears, reminding
one that good still exists.
food comes in its masses,
laid across tables decorated,
seasoned with love,
laughter and mercy from
the precious month passing.
family issues are put to the side
as they sit side to side,
unity and brotherhood,
blood bonds out of friendships
eid at home is a taste of heaven,
if only every other day was just
as beautiful.

- eid.

for the culture

you're from india and i'm from pakistan, your blood is from arabia but still take my hand. you have hair from yemen and those sweedish eyes, a smile from bangladesh and a lebanese charm i cannot lie. you speak swahili and love somalian food, your parents are from kenya, your love resides in morocco. your kindness speaks chinese, your accent is french please. malaysia is where your heart finds home, your british laugh never leaves us alone. indonesia is where you come from, the colour of your skin and the religion we believe in, does not define where we belong. you have kuwaiti henna on your palms, algerian smile but you stay so calm. you're dressed like you belong in nigeria, your happiness covers all of africa. the seven seas carry your faith, from antartica to every single place. don't judge me by my language i speak of the passport i hold, judge me by my manners and the values i hold.

- multicultural love.

draw what comes to your mind when you think of culture:

overthinking

this is the final chapter; this super long read is nearly over. personally, this is my favourite because overthinking is my number one hobby. this chapter just contains random thoughts, the kind of things that will come to your mind when you're trying to sleep but your brain isn't on the same page. this is a compilation of pieces i have found written in the last three years, papers found underneath my bed, random poems at the back of school notebook, quotes scribbled into my notes on my phone. in all honesty it's just random thoughts, those ideas that come to you in the shower or when you're on the tube checking what the guy next to you is doing on his phone. it's just raw poetry and emotion, so let's go.

overthinking

remember those feelings?
they were mine too,
remember those poems i would write you,
remember them tunes we'd vibe too?
love came and i had to invite you
but damn we still fight too,
any lovers might do
and maybe i'll never find anyone like you.

-    remember?

overthinking

our love was made
for another time,
and it breaks me
that i cannot
take you there.

    -    we can only dream.

overthinking

if only you understood my love for the moon,
my words would orbit it for a lifetime.
it will stop chasing the earth
and the sorrow it brings,
it will fall into my arms.

-     moon love.

overthinking

she held the broken
fragments of her
weary soul so
beautifully, i
almost felt like
doing the same
for her.

- why do you break yourself?

overthinking

you held the sun in your
burning arms and the
moon in your chapped
lips.

you were an entire
universe whilst i
was merely a star.

- minuscule

overthinking

everything hurts
without you,
but it's okay
because at night
we both stare
at the same sky,
wishing for
the same things.

-    closer than we believe.

overthinking

your words feel
like the forgotten
hugs of my father
and the fragrance
of my absent mother.

- you give what i crave.

overthinking

i light a cigarette to remember you, to remember how you hated this death i hold in my hands. but i remembered how i promised you i won't smoke anymore, i promised to stop my bad habits and maybe that's why we stopped. so i sat and watched it burn ever so slowly, waiting for the fire to go out, much like the fire you had started within me. you were my first cigarette, you were my first drug and years on i still seem to inhale and let you find home within my lungs. i watched the paper burn, how the ashes flicked out into the night sky, how they disappear the way i did. you are more poisonous than any cigarette, as mine finally died, the fire left, the stench of memories lay thick in the air like a blanket. but you, my aching for your touch does not die, the fire continued to rage, you've got me addicted to a drug i can never have.

- smoke.

overthinking

maybe i could search for
some adjectives to describe
you.

luscious lips, emerald eyes,
soft skin and velvet voice.
but,
hard heart, distant demeanour,
abundant arrogance and lost love.

- adjectives.

overthinking

i guess i'll be okay
maybe i just need to
hurt a little more.
but i hope you have
a good day and don't
feel as lonely as i do,
please hold on,
you're so much stronger.

- please move on,
  i am chaos.

overthinking

the thing is i can see the brokenness in your eyes and your speech is like broken glass. i know you're hurting so please open up to me. i know why you don't want to infect me with the sharpness of your sadness, how your words become razor blades but please why don't you understand it's a sacrifice i am willing to take for you to be okay. let me into your world of sadness, let me build a home within it to shelter you.

- let me in.

overthinking

maybe you aren't the one for me but i'll remember you for eternities, remember you when i'm turning streets, see you in everyone i meet and feel your goodbye in every greet. you left an impression i cannot escape, our love is tattooed in every place, in every expression of every face. i keep falling through every sad song calling, through every fortnight spent bawling, how these thoughts come crawling and how these questions are left stalling, you'll just remain a memory inside, a question mark next to why, an 'at least i tried', but please neither of us lie and say this did not feel like the hardest goodbye.

- acceptance.

overthinking

a year ago
everything seemed so different.
never would i have imagined
life to be like today,
i guess i never understood
how much a year can
do to a person.

- a year ago.

overthinking

sad soul, happy face.
broken heart, full smile.
teary eyes, dry mouth.
trembling hands, still body.
full of feelings, empty of words.
lost mind, found addictions.
empty inside, scarred outside.
numb yet hurting.
every part of me is in conflict,
and i don't know what to do.

-    conflict.

overthinking

may the angels protect you,
may your loved ones accept you.
may peace never neglect you,
may heaven accept you.

- ameen.

overthinking

it's funny how we said we'll continue to be friends and keep on talking but it's been months and i can't bear to hear the words of your name being spoken.

- ironic.

overthinking

you need to understand that too much of anything is bad. too many cigarettes and you die. too much water and you drown. too much love and it becomes destructive. you see, couples don't always end because the love has been lost, or somebody has cheated or distance or all the other million reasons as to why relationships end. sometimes they end because you love one another too much, as absurd as it sounds, and that's scary. you see, that love becomes destructive, it makes you crazy, it strips away your layers of sanity, leaving you in a constant state of intoxication. you end up losing yourself, the love consumes you. you can literally love someone too much, letting it become obsession and hence losing them.

- too much.

overthinking

the worst thing is when you're recovering and things are going well, you're steady and only relapsing now and then but it's more to find sanity than the previous obsession with destruction. but suddenly one thing happens and you're falling and you're falling deeper than you've ever fallen before and you're just scared that you'll end up back at that dark place you fought so hard to escape from. you fear that the darkness will encompass you and absorb into your veins so no longer will you be able to exhale your sadness, meaning you'll eventually choke on your unspoken emotions and lose yourself. i don't want to let that one thing drag me so far back and trip me over after i nearly reached the finishing line.

- tripping.

overthinking

i still miss you.
i'm sorry but at the same time i am not, i keep blaming myself forgetting that you were half of the problem.
how did you leave without looking back?
i hope you find happiness.
sometimes you broke me and i stayed silent because you were the only one who could fix me again.
we live and we learn and i learnt that your love is toxic.
i'm finally happy without you, but sometimes i don't like it.
i still don't know how we lost it all.
i'm not okay.
there are days i see you everywhere, i'd be lying if i said i hated it.

- everything i wish i told you.

overthinking

if there ever was a paradise
in this broken world,
it would be you, mother.
for your sadness makes me
forget the harshness of the
dunya. may happiness always
befall you, may gardens of
green blossom in your presence.
may sadness run at the sound
of your gentle voice, and may
my smile become yours.

- this one is for you.

overthinking

1.) your heart will break but you are more than just a heart so you won't. your limbs will carry you strong, your soul will push you up, your tongue will clear pathways and your eyes will guide you. don't let your heart control you.

2.) don't believe every i love you that pierces your skin and befriends your sadness. we mistake love for lust and lust for love, no-one can heal your sadness except for you, don't find another to complete you.

3.) the world is harsh but darling it was never here to break you, listen to the winds and flirt with the moonlight, they are here to love. the world will enlighten you, it will heal your aching bones after it breaks them.

4.) don't lose who you are, please.

5.) someone will come and make your pain taste like honey but don't fall for the sweetness of their lies, everything that looks sweet doesn't taste it.

- five things i wish i was told.

overthinking

when i say i am tired, i'm not physically tired, it's just that my worries are weighing so hard down on my chest that every breath feels like a dagger in my chest and all i want to do is lie in my bed in the dark and cry a little and then turn to my side and overthink everything.

yes it sounds ever so horrible and destructive, to isolate yourself and create these scenarios within your head that will never happen but sometimes that's all that makes me okay.

- my chaos leads me to clarity.

overthinking

your home of love and care,
of family laughter and smiles,
your home where happiness we hear,
has been gone for a while.
your tower fell and it wasn't your fault,
government failures are to blame,
your sadness bought my city to a halt,
in my prayers i mention your name.
i'm sorry there's no answers left,
that your hearts are broken,
but i promise to try my best,
to give back the hope that was stolen.
your courage will inspire us forever,
your bravery will be praised,
for now a community stands together,
so the next can be saved.

- grenfell.

overthinking

for you,
sweet child.
you are born into a world,
a beautiful little girl,
with bright brown eyes,
and a candid smile.
this world my beloved
is littered with fears,
but the least i can promise,
is that i'll silence your tears.
you are so innocent,
so fragile and soft,
so hold my hand,
clutch it tight,
and with your family
you'll never be lost.

> \-   for you, anna sofiya,
> may god bless you
> with all the love
> and happiness in
> this world, and unite
> us in the hereafter
> too.

\-

overthinking

the thing is, this book doesn't end.
i pray these words and emotions stay
with you through your good days
and your bad days. that when you
feel lost, my words give you comfort,
fall in love, laugh, cry, hope, that's
what i want my words to do.

-    finale.

thank you for getting to the end, for reading my thoughts, my emotions, the good days, bad days, the love, the breaking, the recovery, the messy bits and the bits where i try to help.

thank you once again to everyone, to all my loved ones, you know who you are. to my special ones, the friends I have made, the loved ones i have lost. without the losses and gains in my life i would not have wrote this book. for my other half, wherever you are, i pray you read this book and fall in love with the words, and more with the author.

i'm going to leave you guys with one final quote, or more of a thought for us all to ponder upon.

> *there are many things in life we can postpone,*
> *love is one, healing is another,*
> *but pain, it comes at its perfect time.*
> - *thesmilingakh*

contact:

instagram: @thesmilingakh
twitter: @thesmilingakh
email: thesmilingakh@gmail.com

keep strong, keep faith, you're going to be okay. if you're looking for a sign, this is your sign, this is your sign telling you that you are gonna find so much happiness that you'll forget what sadness feels lie.

keep me in your prayers. may peace and blessings be upon you all.